MAKING

THUNDER
WINGS

FROM JUNK

FROM JUNK

Chocks away! With Tech-Nick and the rest of the squad you'll soon be off the ground with five of your very own Thunder Wing planes.

Nick, RT-1, Databot and Nano will show you exactly how to turn recycled parts, from around the home, into some of the sleekest aircraft around.

Parts In this section you will find photos of all the parts you'll need to collect, plus tips on finding alternatives to the ones shown.

Painting Learn all about adding great paint effects and finishing touches - plus ideas on applying the stickers found in the back of this book.

Assembly This section will show you how to construct each of the five Thunder Wings in this book using simple step by step instructions.

Red Alert Watch out for safety alerts, especially when using sharp tools. Always ask an adult for help when advised to do so.

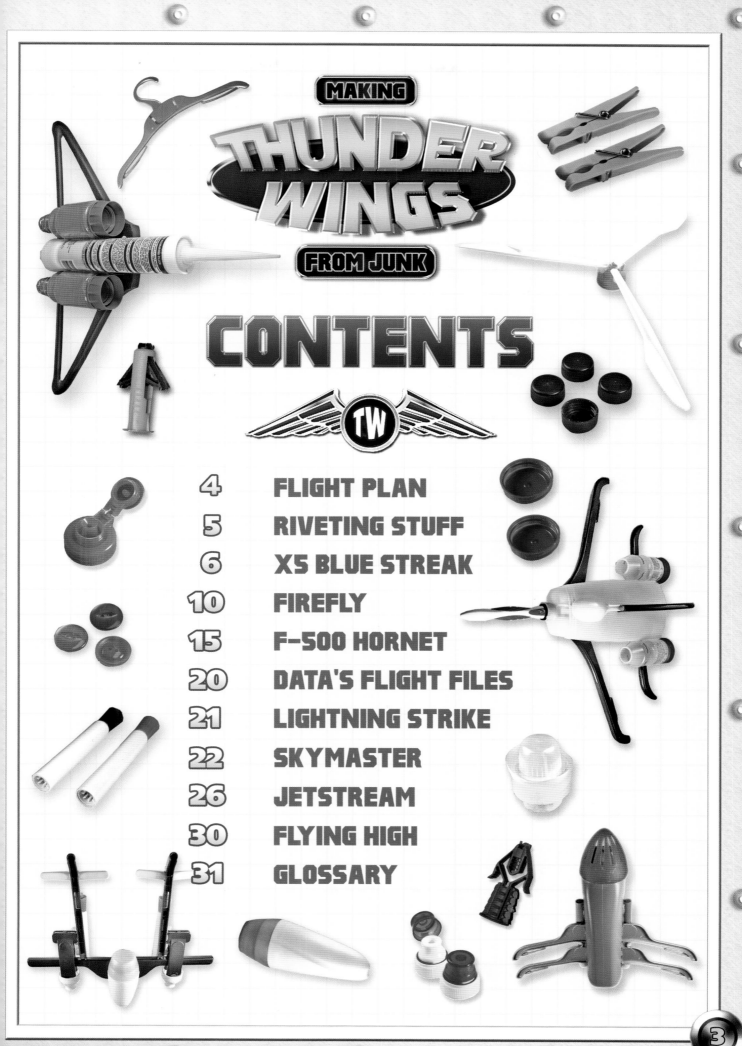

MAKING
THUNDER WINGS
FROM JUNK

CONTENTS

TW

FLIGHT PLAN

Get off to a flying start by collecting all those plastic throw-aways from around the home, then locate the tools shown on each page and find a place to start junk crafting.

Ask friends and family to collect for you - especially if there are products shown in this book that you don't normally buy. You'll be encouraging them to recycle too.

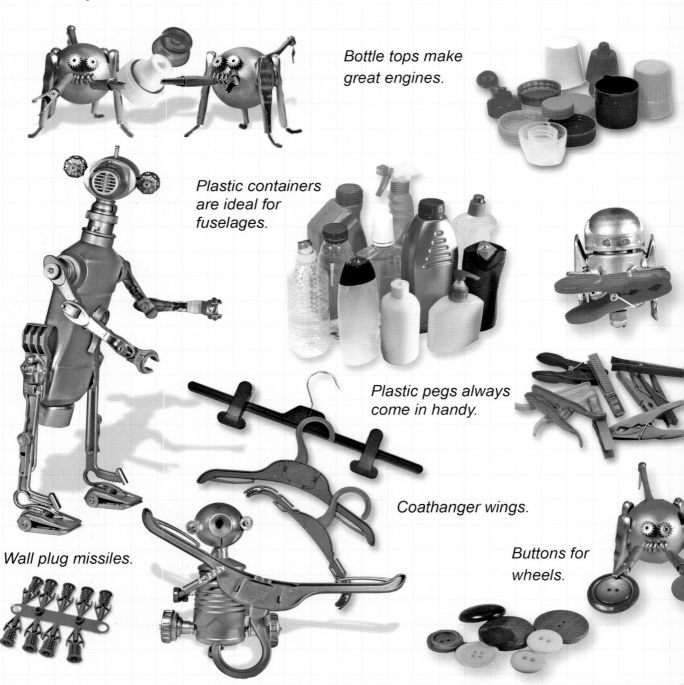

Bottle tops make great engines.

Plastic containers are ideal for fuselages.

Plastic pegs always come in handy.

Coathanger wings.

Wall plug missiles.

Buttons for wheels.

Real planes are held together with nuts, bolts and rivets. For your Thunder Wing aircraft use strong glue - or, better still, a glue gun.

This device heats up a stick of glue until it is runny enough to squirt where you want it. As the glue cools it sets hard and strong. Ask an adult for help when using one and always wear rubber gloves to protect your hands from hot glue.

USE RUBBER KITCHEN GLOVES OR PROTECTIVE DIY GLOVES

Hot Melt
Glue Sticks

Plastic coathangers and pegs may need to be cut in order to build your aircraft. Use a small junior hacksaw and rest on a firm workbench.

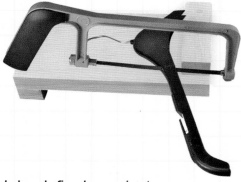

A bench hook is a block of wood with a lip on each side - one to hold it firmly against the edge of a table, and the other to hold your workpiece in place whilst cutting.

Hold the bench hook firmly against the edge of a work table and saw gently.

Saw teeth face forwards so they cut as you push.

Powered by two ramjet engines, the X-5 is capable of speeds of up to three times the speed of sound.

One hacksaw cut and nine squirts of glue are all that's needed.

Blue Streak can outrun any other plane in the skies and can reach altitudes on the very edge of space.

TOOLS

Junior Hacksaw

Glue Gun or Strong Glue

GLUE

Always wear gloves when using a glue gun.

PARTS

Two large fresh juice bottles tops

Two small juice bottle

Large plastic hanger

Two plastic knives

Empty decorator's filler tube

CAULK DECORATORS FILLER
MULTI-PURPOSE

Plastic peg

Top from a large fabric conditioner bottle

1 Saw the metal hook from the large plastic hanger with a junior hacksaw.

! *Rest on a firm workbench when cutting.*

2 Glue the fabric conditioner top to the open end of the decorator's filler tube.

3 Glue the decorator's filler tube fuselage to the hanger.

4 Glue a fresh juice bottle top to the bottom of each juice bottle to create the engines.

5 Glue the engines to the sides of the fuselage as shown.

6 Twist apart the two halves of a plastic peg.

7 Glue the two peg halves and two plastic knives to the top of the fuselage as fins and cockpit canopy.

8 Follow steps 12 to 14 on page 18 to make these undercarriage wheels for the X-5.

TO MAKE THE WHEELS YOU WILL NEED THREE BUTTONS AND THREE PEGS

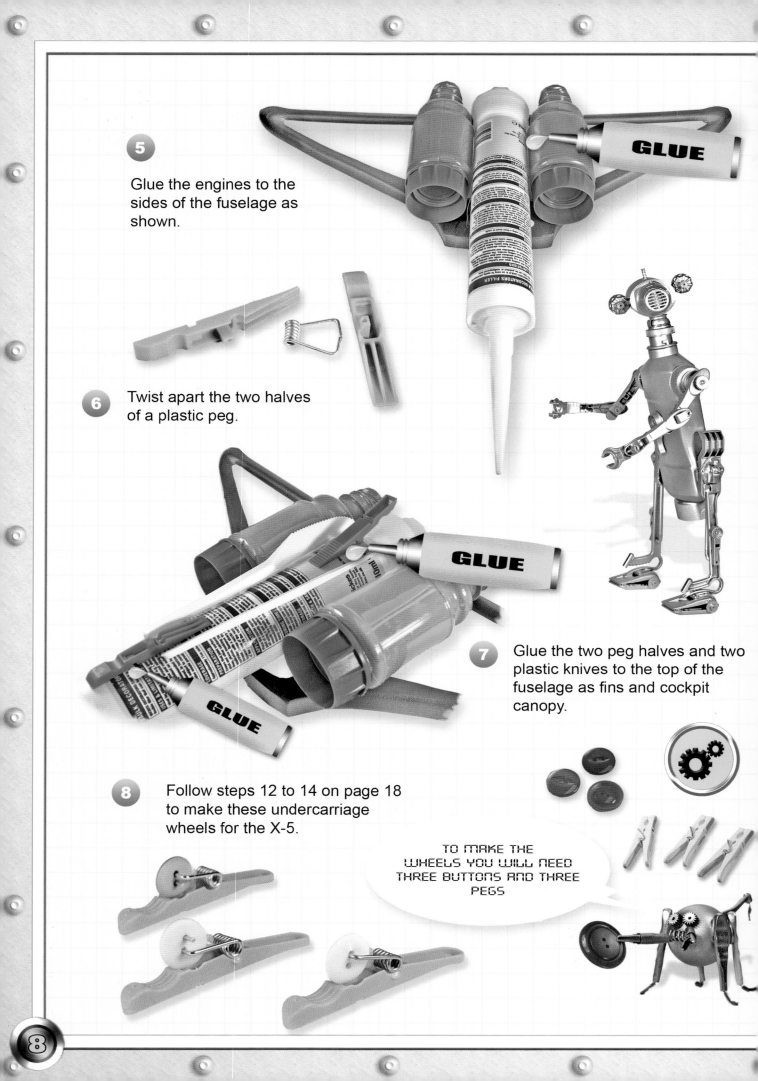

Use acrylic spray paints to give your Thunder Wings a great look. Use metallic silver or grey primer.
It dries quickly and leaves a smooth even finish.

Spray in short bursts and keep the can moving to avoid runs.

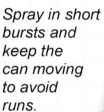

Hang Blue Streak from an outside line using string or strong thread.

Attach the undercarriage wheels and paint with black acrylic paint. To add the missiles shown below, check out page 21.

When it comes to agility and manoeverability, Firefly is hard to beat.

With three blades and a jet thruster, this little chopper can hover and dart like a dragonfly on fire.

Collect together all the parts and tools shown on this page and ask an adult for help when recommended.

PARTS

Washing up liquid bottle top

Trigger action spray bottle top

Long and short plastic hangers

Three plastic knives

Wooden barbecue skewer

TOOLS

Bradawl

Junior Hacksaw

Tealight and Matches

Glue Gun or Strong Glue

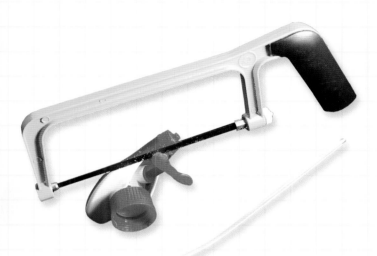

1 Pull out the plastic tube from the spray bottle top and saw off the trigger with a junior hacksaw.

GLUE

2 If the spray bottle top has a rotating collar, glue around the top of it to fix it firmly in place.

KEEP THE TRIGGER IN A SAFE PLACE - YOU WILL NEED IT AT STEP 16

3 Saw one arm from the large plastic hanger with a junior hacksaw.

GLUE

Use strong glue to attach the tail and leave it to set thoroughly.

4 Glue the sawn-off arm of the hanger to the nozzle of the spray bottle top.

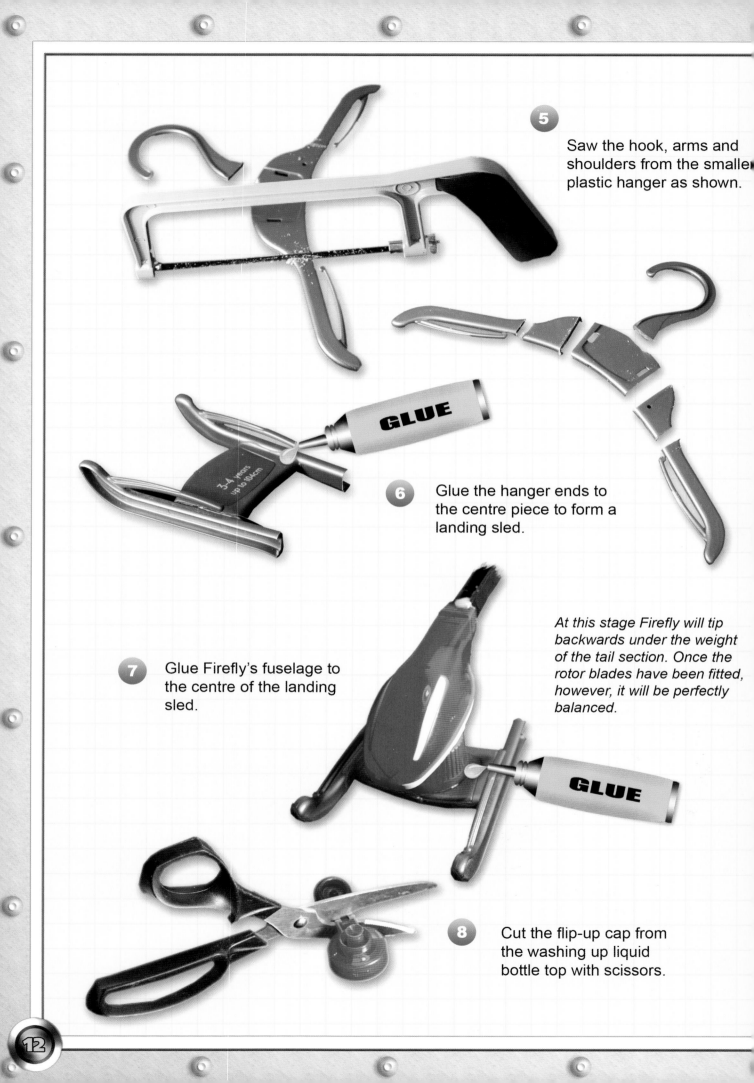

5 Saw the hook, arms and shoulders from the smaller plastic hanger as shown.

6 Glue the hanger ends to the centre piece to form a landing sled.

7 Glue Firefly's fuselage to the centre of the landing sled.

At this stage Firefly will tip backwards under the weight of the tail section. Once the rotor blades have been fitted, however, it will be perfectly balanced.

8 Cut the flip-up cap from the washing up liquid bottle top with scissors.

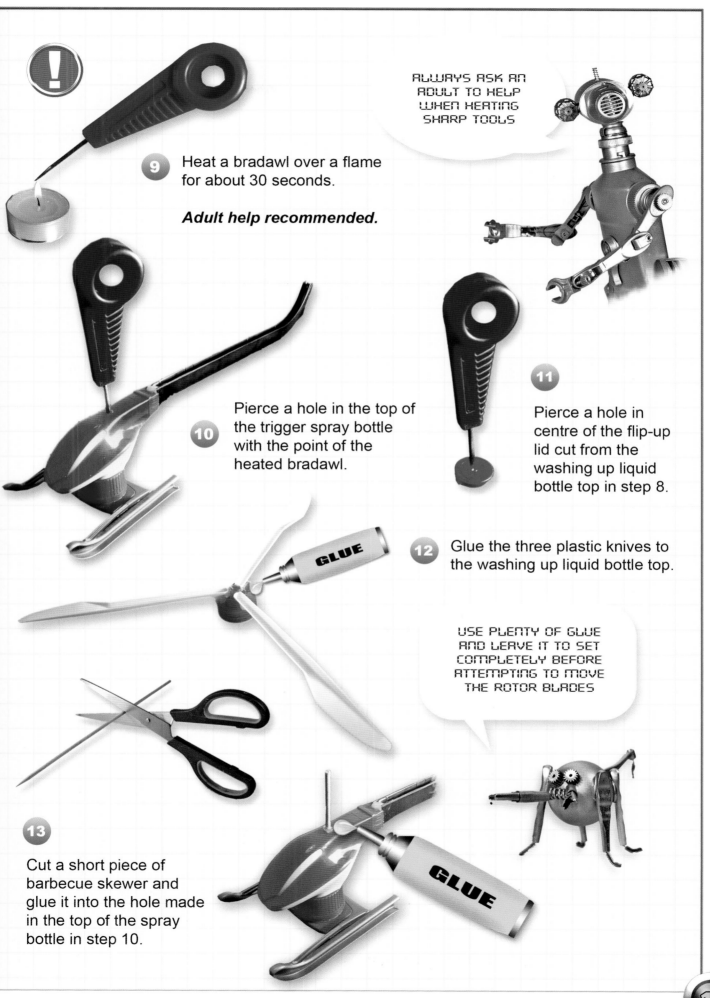

9 Heat a bradawl over a flame for about 30 seconds.

Adult help recommended.

10 Pierce a hole in the top of the trigger spray bottle with the point of the heated bradawl.

11 Pierce a hole in centre of the flip-up lid cut from the washing up liquid bottle top in step 8.

GLUE

12 Glue the three plastic knives to the washing up liquid bottle top.

13 Cut a short piece of barbecue skewer and glue it into the hole made in the top of the spray bottle in step 10.

GLUE

14

Slide the rotor blade assembly onto the barbecue skewer spindle.

15

Glue the cap from the washing up liquid bottle to the top of the rotor spindle, upside down.

GLUE

Take care not to get any glue on the rotor blade assembly.

GLUE

16

Glue the trigger from the spray bottle top to the tail of Firefly for a stabiliser.

The blades should rotate freely when you spin them.

You may decide not to spray Firefly if it is already the colour you want.

Use the black and white striped stickers to decorate the rotors or tail.

FIREFLY
6513D

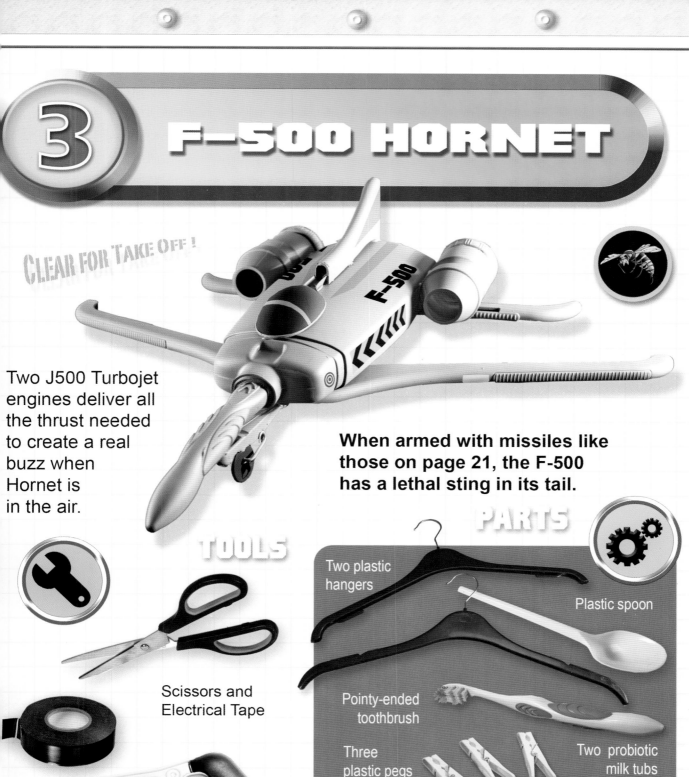

CLEAR FOR TAKE OFF !

Two J500 Turbojet engines deliver all the thrust needed to create a real buzz when Hornet is in the air.

When armed with missiles like those on page 21, the F-500 has a lethal sting in its tail.

TOOLS

Scissors and Electrical Tape

Junior Hacksaw

GLUE

Glue Gun or Strong Glue

Always wear rubber gloves when using a glue gun.

PARTS

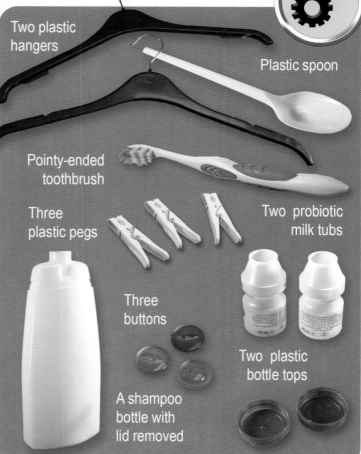

Two plastic hangers

Plastic spoon

Pointy-ended toothbrush

Three plastic pegs

Two probiotic milk tubs

Three buttons

Two plastic bottle tops

A shampoo bottle with lid removed

1 Cut the hook from one of the plastic hangers with a junior hacksaw.

2 Glue the hanger to the shampoo bottle as shown.

3 Glue the probiotic milk tubs to the sides of the shampoo bottle as engines.

GLUE

GLUE

ALWAYS REST ON A FIRM WORKSURFACE WHEN CUTTING

4 Saw the second plastic hanger into four sections with a junior hacksaw as shown.

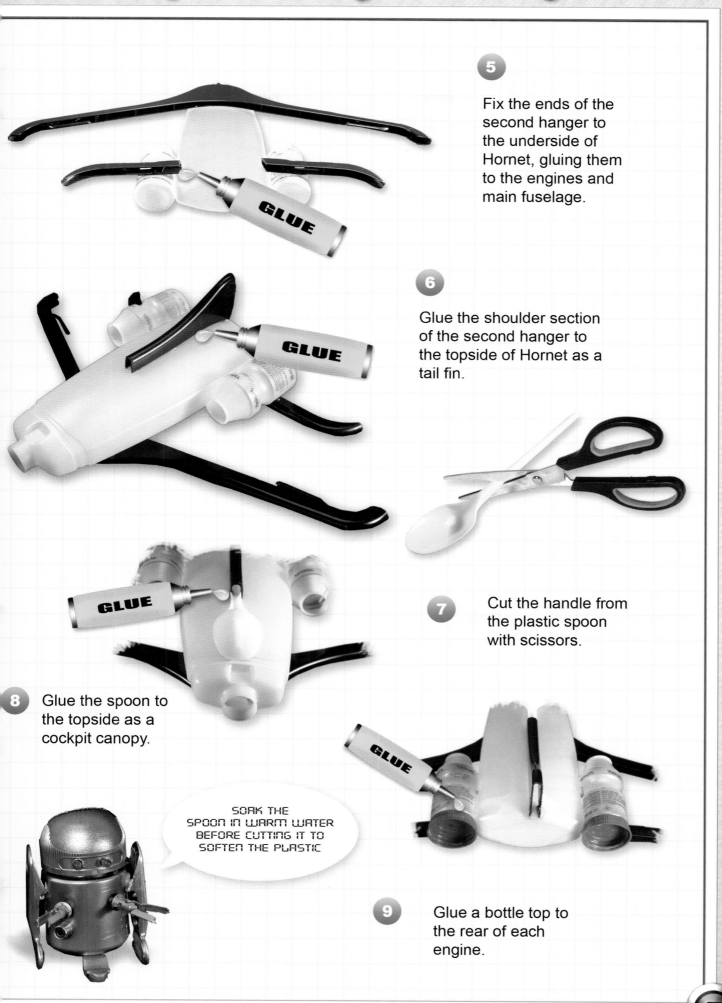

5 Fix the ends of the second hanger to the underside of Hornet, gluing them to the engines and main fuselage.

6 Glue the shoulder section of the second hanger to the topside of Hornet as a tail fin.

7 Cut the handle from the plastic spoon with scissors.

8 Glue the spoon to the topside as a cockpit canopy.

SOAK THE SPOON IN WARM WATER BEFORE CUTTING IT TO SOFTEN THE PLASTIC

9 Glue a bottle top to the rear of each engine.

10 Wrap electrical tape around the handle of the toothbrush until it is wide enough to fit tightly into the neck of the shampoo bottle.

About 25 turns should do it.

11 Push the toothbrush into the top of the shampoo bottle - adding or removing tape until it fits just right.

12 Pull the pegs apart.

13 Fit the ends of a spring through the holes of each of the three buttons.

GLUE

14 Glue each wheel to a peg half to form the undercarriage.

15 Glue one undercarriage assembly to the front and two to the rear of Hornet's underside.

GLUE

GLUE

243

F-500

Spray Paint

Spray Hornet grey or silver, then paint the wheels and canopy black and add stickers.

Hang your finished aircraft from a washing line and spray with short bursts of paint.

Spray
Paint

LET THE PAINT DRY
BEFORE ADDING MORE
LAYERS

Spray
Paint

Spray outdoors or in a well ventilated work room.

If you can't use an outside line, make a spray booth by turning a cardboard box on its side.

Position these hot stickers in Hornet's engine outlets.

DATA'S FLIGHT FILES

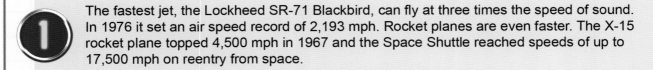

Check out Databot's top aviation facts

1 The fastest jet, the Lockheed SR-71 Blackbird, can fly at three times the speed of sound. In 1976 it set an air speed record of 2,193 mph. Rocket planes are even faster. The X-15 rocket plane topped 4,500 mph in 1967 and the Space Shuttle reached speeds of up to 17,500 mph on reentry from space.

2 The Hughes H-4 Hercules, or Spruce Goose, had the longest wings of any plane in history, almost 100 metres from wingtip to wingtip. It made just one flight in November 1947. The Stratolaunch Carrier Aircraft is still being designed, but when built, will have a wingspan of 117 metres. Powered by six Jumbo Jet engines, it will launch spacecraft into orbit.

3 Bicycle-making brothers, Orville and Wilbur Wright were the first to build and fly a controllable heavier than air flying machine. Their first flight was at Kill Devil Hill in North Carolina, USA, on December 17th 1903. Orville, the pilot, stayed airborne for 12 seconds, covering a distance of 37 metres.

4 The Heinkel He 178 was the first ever turbojet aircraft. It was first flown in August 1939 by Flight Captain Erich Warsitz, reaching a maximum speed of 380 mph. Flight Captain Warsitz also flew a rocket-powered plane, the Heinkel He 176, that same year.

5 The first around the world flight was by six United States aviators who travelled a distance of 27,000 miles in three Douglas DT-2 biplanes. They set off from Seattle, Washington, on March 17th 1924 and arrived back 175 days later.

6 The highest a jet plane has ever flown is just over 37,600 metres. It was reached by a Russian MIG-25 Foxbat in 1977. In 2004 a rocket plane, SpaceshipOne, was launched from its mothership, White Knight, and reached an altitude of almost 112,000 metres.

7 Gyroplane Number One was the first manned helicopter to get off the ground. Designed and built by the French Breguet brothers, it only rose half a metre in the air for one minute on its maiden flight in September 1907. One of the brothers, Louis Breguet, went on to design other flying machines and achieved an altitude of 158 metres in 1935 with his Gyroplane Laboratoire.

8 The Dornier DO X had a total of twelve piston engines, and that's a record. Six propellers faced backwards and were designed to push - while the other six, facing forwards, pulled the massive seaplane through the air. When it comes to jet engines, the Boeing B-52 Stratofortress takes second place with an engine count of eight turbofans and a fuel tank that can hold 182,000 litres.

9 The Harrier Jump Jet is a V/STOL (Vertical/ Short take off and landing) aircraft that uses one Rolls Royce Pegasus Turbofan engine with four rotating thruster nozzles to fly in any direction or hover, just like a humming bird. The all-new F-35B Lightning II has short take off and vertical landing capability.

10 Stealth aircraft, including the F-117 Nighthawk and the B-2 Spirit, are designed to avoid being spotted by the enemy. Their wings are covered with non-metallic materials with flat surfaces to deflect Radar and radio waves. Engines and weapons are hidden within the aircraft and bombs are only revealed at the very last moment.

LIGHTNING STRIKE

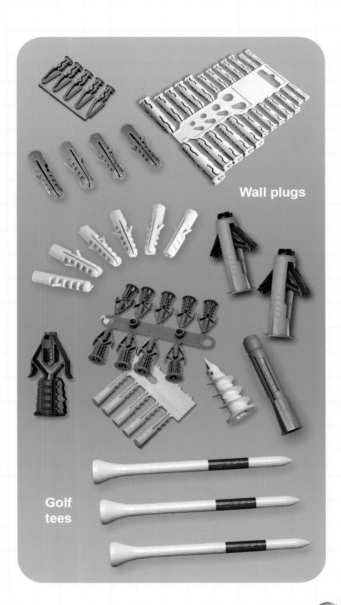

Wall plugs

Golf tees

Use wall plugs and other small parts to make missiles and bombs for your Thunder Wings.

Glue them on just as they are, or combine them to make awesome weaponry.

GLUE

Glue weapons along the underside of your Thunder Wings and paint them for an authentic look.

GLUE

Skymaster is a twin-tailed, twin turbo jet plane that lands on water - the perfect jet for getting to small islands where there are no runways.

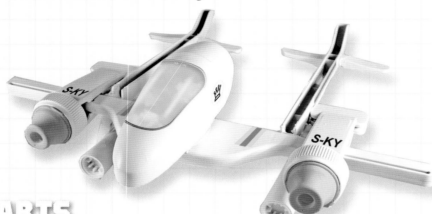

It can seat six and has a range of five hundred miles.

With a wide cockpit canopy, passengers enjoy a great view all round.

PARTS

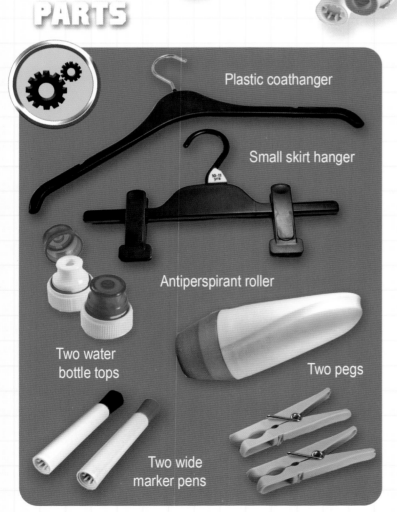

Plastic coathanger

Small skirt hanger

Antiperspirant roller

Two water bottle tops

Two pegs

Two wide marker pens

TOOLS

Scissors

Junior Hacksaw

Glue Gun or Strong Glue

GLUE

ASSEMBLY WORKSHOP

1 Cut the hook from the plastic skirt hanger with a junior hacksaw.

2 Glue the antiperspirant dispenser to the skirt hanger as shown.

3 Cut the arms from the plastic coathanger with the hacksaw.

Push the clips right in.

LEAVE THE GLUE TO SET BEFORE MOVING SKYMASTER

4 Make sure that the hanger clips are pushed in as far as possible, then fix each tail section in place with glue.

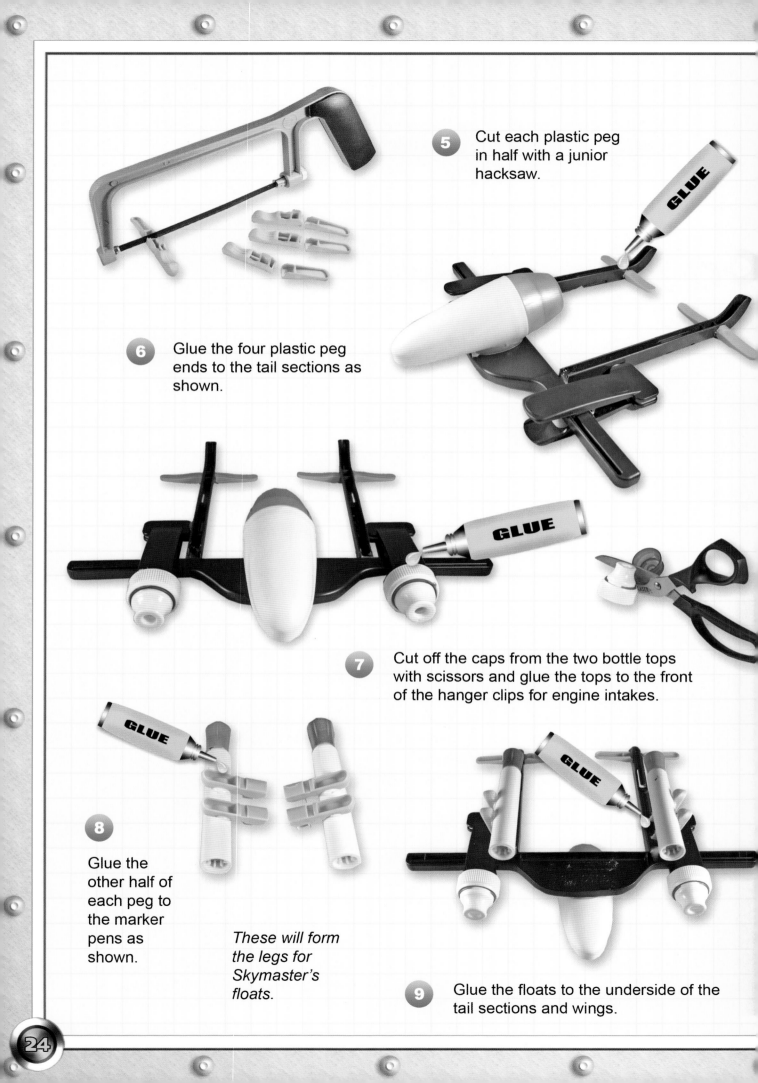

5 Cut each plastic peg in half with a junior hacksaw.

6 Glue the four plastic peg ends to the tail sections as shown.

7 Cut off the caps from the two bottle tops with scissors and glue the tops to the front of the hanger clips for engine intakes.

8 Glue the other half of each peg to the marker pens as shown.

These will form the legs for Skymaster's floats.

9 Glue the floats to the underside of the tail sections and wings.

Use spray paints to give your Skymaster an overall colour then add the stickers found in the back of this book.

CS 126012

SKYMASTER

White primer paint gives an even matt finish.

It is also less likely to run than gloss paint.

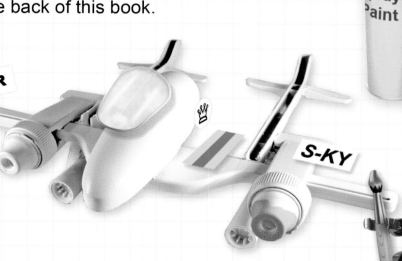

S-KY

Paint the engine intakes with bright acrylic paint.

RT-1

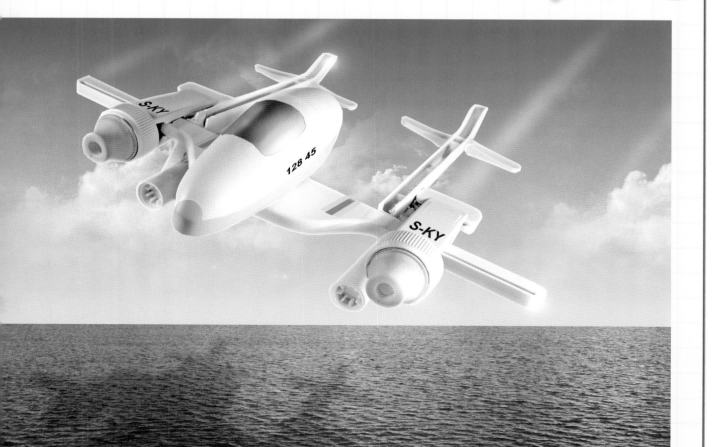

S-KY

128 45

S-KY

5 JET STREAM

Versatile and reliable, Jet Stream can be adapted for a whole range of vital roles.

Equipped with state of the art medical equipment, it serves as an air ambulance.

With space in the back for cargo or passengers, Jet Stream can act as a courier plane or a private jet.

PARTS

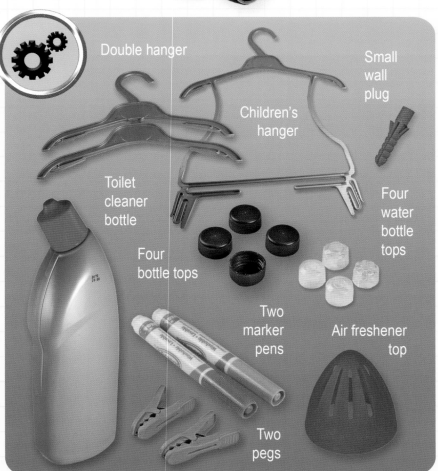

- Double hanger
- Children's hanger
- Small wall plug
- Toilet cleaner bottle
- Four bottle tops
- Four water bottle tops
- Two marker pens
- Air freshener top
- Two pegs

TOOLS

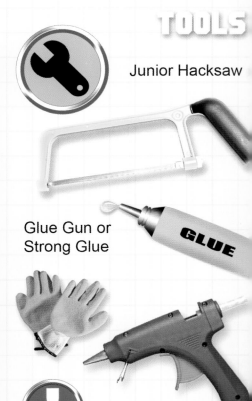

Junior Hacksaw

Glue Gun or Strong Glue

Always wear gloves when using a glue gun.

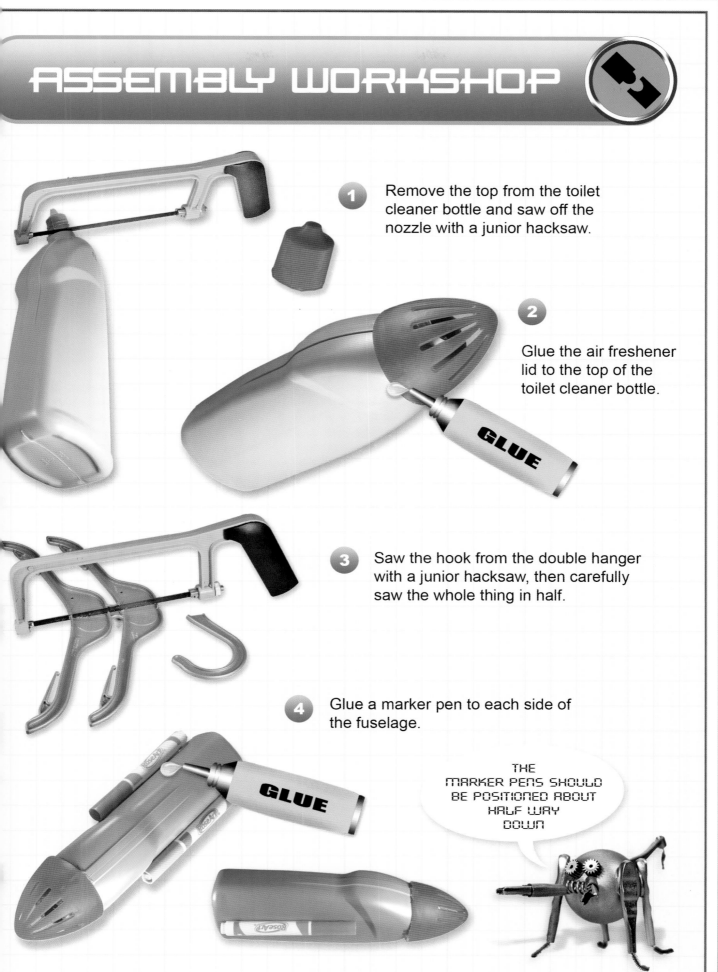

1 Remove the top from the toilet cleaner bottle and saw off the nozzle with a junior hacksaw.

2 Glue the air freshener lid to the top of the toilet cleaner bottle.

GLUE

3 Saw the hook from the double hanger with a junior hacksaw, then carefully saw the whole thing in half.

4 Glue a marker pen to each side of the fuselage.

GLUE

THE MARKER PENS SHOULD BE POSITIONED ABOUT HALF WAY DOWN

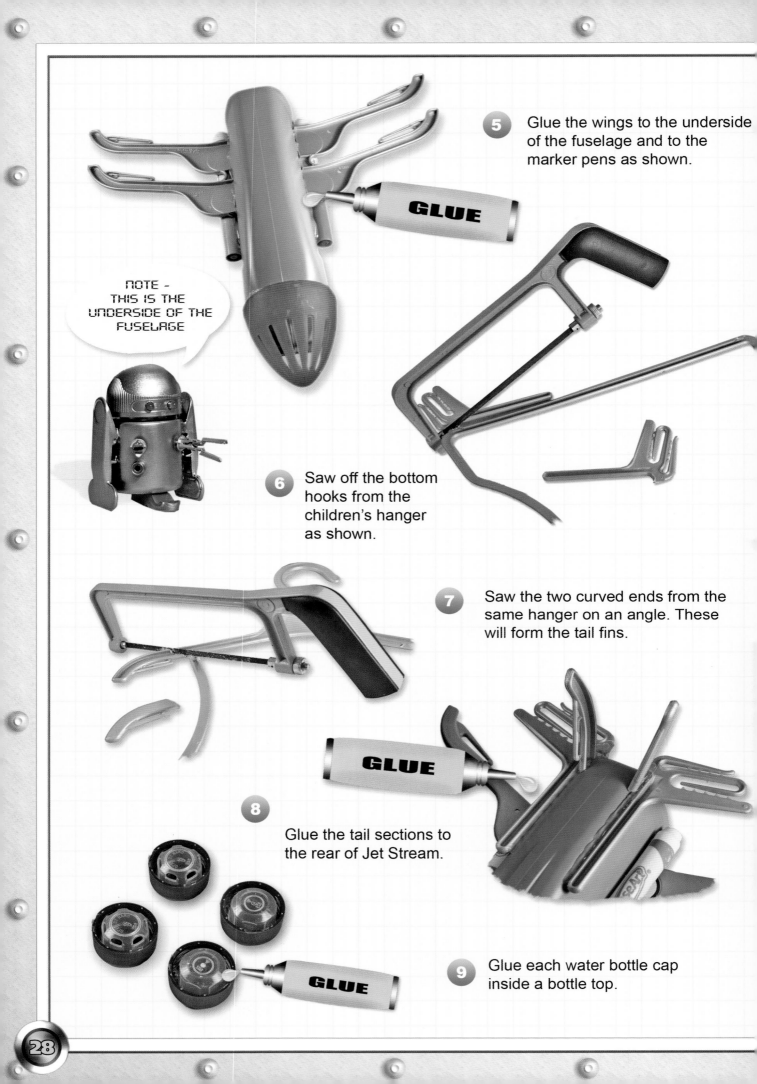

5 Glue the wings to the underside of the fuselage and to the marker pens as shown.

GLUE

NOTE -
THIS IS THE
UNDERSIDE OF THE
FUSELAGE

6 Saw off the bottom hooks from the children's hanger as shown.

7 Saw the two curved ends from the same hanger on an angle. These will form the tail fins.

GLUE

8 Glue the tail sections to the rear of Jet Stream.

9 Glue each water bottle cap inside a bottle top.

GLUE

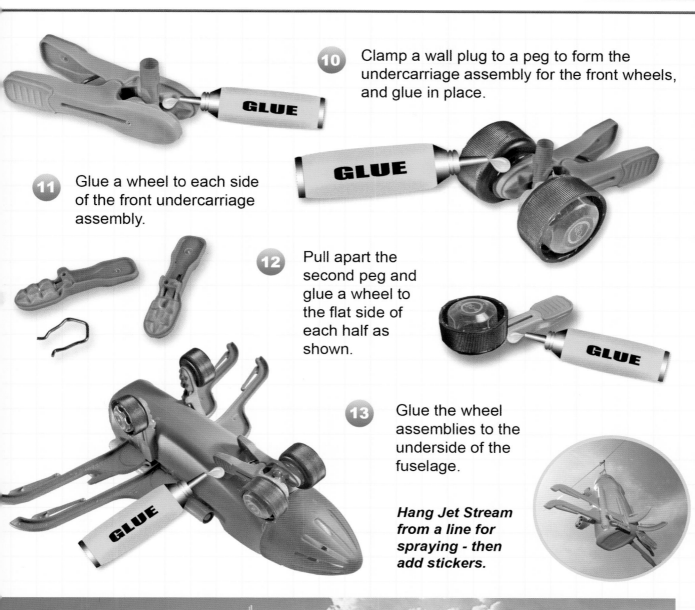

10 Clamp a wall plug to a peg to form the undercarriage assembly for the front wheels, and glue in place.

11 Glue a wheel to each side of the front undercarriage assembly.

12 Pull apart the second peg and glue a wheel to the flat side of each half as shown.

13 Glue the wheel assemblies to the underside of the fuselage.

Hang Jet Stream from a line for spraying - then add stickers.

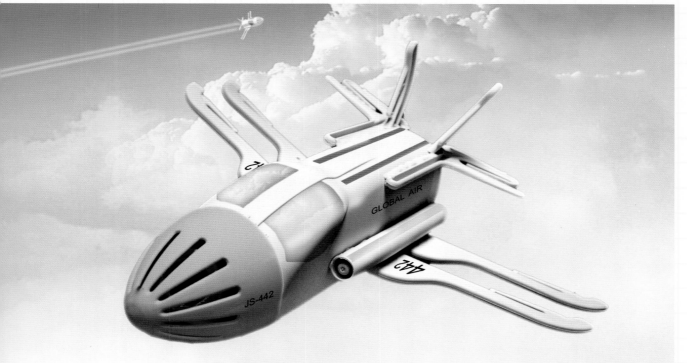

FLYING HIGH

Once you have built and painted your Thunder Wing aircraft, try these methods of putting them on display.

You will need fishing line, or strong thread as well as offcuts of wood.

Use nylon line or strong thread to hang your planes from the ceiling.

1 *Heat the tip of a bradawl over a tealight and pierce a hole in the underside of the aircraft for a rod to fit into.*

Make a stand using an offcut of wood and a rod.

2 *Drill a thin hole in a circle or square of wood for the other end of the rod or skewer.*

3 *Bend a piece of coathanger wire or use a barbecue skewer to mount your plane on the base.*

Display your Thunder Wings on a rectangle of board, painted to look like a section of runway.

Stone-effect spray paint is ideal.

GLOSSARY

Acrylic paint
Fast drying paint that can be diluted in water, but is waterproof when dry.

Altitude
Height above sea level.

Antiperspirant
A chemical you put on the skin to reduce sweating.

Barbecue skewers
Long thin sticks of wood used for holding pieces of meat together whilst cooking.

Biplane
An aeroplane that has two sets of wings, one above the other.

Cockpit Canopy
The glass window that covers the seat where the pilot sits.

Electrical tape
Stretchy plastic sticky tape used by electricians to wrap around wires.

Fuselage
The main body of an aeroplane to which the wings and tail are normally attached.

Mach Speed
The speed of an aeroplane compared to the speed of sound. Mach 1 is the speed of sound. Mach 2 is twice that speed.

Propeller
The rotating blades of a piston-engined plane.

Radar
A device that sends and receives radio waves for detecting enemy planes. It stands for **Ra**dio **D**etecting **A**nd **R**anging.

Ramjet
A jet engine that uses the forward speed of the plane to force air into the engine.

Recycle
To reuse waste materials or to change them in some way for another purpose.

Stealth plane
An aircraft that uses special means to avoid detection by the enemy.

Supersonic
Faster than the speed of sound waves through air.

Turbojet
A jet engine that uses rotating turbines to compress air before burning it.

Undercarriage
Parts of the aircraft that are below the body, especially the wheels.

Wingspan
The distance from wingtip to wingtip.

First published in Great Britain in 2012 by Junkcraft Books. Email info@junkcraft.com
Text and Images © Junkcraft Books 2012. Stephen Munzer has asserted his rights under the Copyright, Designs and Patents Act, 1988, to be identified as the author of this work.
All rights reserved. No part of this publication may be reproduced or transmitted or utilised in any form or by any means, electronic, mechanical, or otherwise, without prior permission of the publisher.

Designed and produced exclusively for Junkcraft Books.
Printed and Bound by Everbest Printing Co Ltd, China.

A CIP catalogue record for this book is available from the British Library.
ISBN 978-0-9571566-2-3

www.junkcraft.com